Kalamazoo
August 1, 1983

For Trudy,
remembering two wild weeks
at Oxbow — paper, people,
and poems —
affectionately,
Marion and Con

rust

rust

Conrad Hilberry

Conrad Hilberry

Ohio University Press, Athens

For Marion, Marilyn, Jane, and Ann

Acknowledgments

Beloit Poetry Journal
Contempora
Eclat
Field
Hiram Poetry Review
Ironwood
Michigan Hot Apples
Michigan Signatures
New York *Times*
Poetry Northwest
Sumac
34th Street
Westigan Review

I wish to thank
the Chapelbrook Foundation for a grant
which provided time to write
a number of these poems.

Contents

one

1   Fourteen days ago, the sun lost
His footing and fell in a drainage
Ditch. I can show you the place—
A stubble field near Schoolcraft. Today
Sleet peppers him from above and cornstalks
And marsh grass give him a cold
Finger from below. He might as well
Roll up in the bullrushes
And wait it out.

This morning a hawk
Flew low behind the house,
His hooks out, dragging the dark air,
Hunting the right life for himself.

2   Nothing was settled
In summer, when
Children played kickball
And chimney swifts tumbled
And dipped in the last light.
A boy drew long roots of air
Into his harmonica, tasting
Them, packing them with his hands.
When he blew, a tree
Big as the street
Trembled out of his mouth.

3   I can follow a scent in this weather.
My eyes narrow to points,
Feet and hands turn leather.
I know where I'm going for once.

I run a knife from the chin
To the crotch and ease
Back the hairy skin.
I stuff a deepfreeze.

4   In Indochina, the hawks
Go in low and sure,
Cutting the roads, cutting
The bodies of bicyclers
Who weave slowly south.
Reconnaisance planes look
Everywhere with their
Long eyes.

5   When I think of summer
I think of falling
Water and the salt
Of my body washing away.

6   I can tell you what it is
To be lost
In the mountains: reticence
Of trees and the hard
Rush of water.

Deeper and deeper in,
The stream taking you
A strange way. Feet
In the water,
You slip from the dark
Side of stones.
Afraid. The gentle
Teeth of the fern
Have eaten your
Going back.

You ask the way at each
Turning, and are answered
Birch, basswood,
Water over a rock.

This is lawyer's weather.
A dog digs for cold bones.
Rock salt runs a fever
Cutting down to the stones.

Certainty has a price:
We notarize our wives.
Sweet Mother of Christ,
Let the sun rise.

7

A river rattles its money
In the dark. A crow coughs.
Lightning talks low over the Adirondacks.
Pines let their needles fall,
The first drops of rain.

You sleep in flat country.
I miss your gullies, the cricket
Music of your legs.

This is the last of the plums
You sent with me. I hold
The pit in my hand,
Seed out of its flesh.

A red fox rolls
In the fern, head back,
Crying out of the soft fur
Of its throat. A rabbit
Nibbles the watercress.
Your breasts hold their fire.

Wait. This is no place for poems.
In the damp, they grow
Luxuriant, soft-edged,
Not to be trusted: the breasts
Are real, the animals made up.
We swim in a hopeless twist
Of touch and taste—let someone
Else's poems harden in the sun.

The stream in this green wood
Washes boulders with a smooth
Hand, lays bare the roots
Of the beech tree. A tongue
Can drink here without words.

Public eyes look out
From the sound proofed ceiling.
A squad of chairs present themselves,
Heads back, elbows linked.   A Toronado
Revolves, but the open doors reveal
Vinyl and the usual apparatus.

"Trans-World Airlines Jet Stream Service for Los Angeles
now boarding at Gate 36.   All aboard, please."   The voice
eases up and down as if she were administering
artificial insemination.

Suddenly, grass leans in
Where the door is ajar,
Moss greens the north
Side of pillars.

That is to say, a fat young priest in green
Glasses and grey suit, poses with his pipe,
Clerical—then, weakening, slips a dime in a machine
And peels Mr. Goodbar out of his wrap.

Dandelions, tendrils of morning glory.
Even the tapered overcoat is crowned
By a hat natty as a sunflower
On top of the National Bank.

Outside the window, prodigious jets rise to a pricking
angle and ease into the sky.

Coming in, a soldier hugs
His father, a huge man smiling
In his flesh. Blooms of ninebark, sparrows, tohees.
A man in a jacket opens a cigarette machine
And stoops to reload. A small Italian
With a thermos of coffee, he counts packs
Of Kools in a tunnel of Muzak.

Underfoot the terrazzo stirs, gravel
Shifting with the current. I move
To Gate 36 in a school of travellers,
Our feet flashing in the new water.

I
A gravel road crosses into the sand burrs
Pulling its wires
Over a low hill, hanging
Black tracks in the sky.

Those tracks: the rise and fade of voices
Stretching out behind. Two mourning
Doves and a grackle
Listen with their feet.

II
Do you remember in department stores
The tubes whistling their breath in,
The $5 bill stuffed in a cylinder and sucked
Up to the cashier in a glass box?

                                   These tracks
Suck us into the dark of Union Station
Marking nothing we have thought or said;
The claws of the curious birds
Can get no purchase on the rails.

1
> My daughters make wheel and spokes
> In the snow of the park:
> One fox, two geese. At 4:30
> It is dusk. An early moon watches
> The game with half an eye.

2
> March 1. My number: 108. Called
> Except for a steel hip
> And 41 spruce trees
> 41 hamburger buns skidding for grackles on snow crust
> 41 daughters, wives
> 41 bicycle tubes patched and pumped
> 41 pork loins @ 89¢
> 41 Yeats poems ranting and carolling in a mad tenor.

3
> I hung at the sky's end
> Of a seesaw one summer, then
> Down while my brother rose,
> A kite taking the wind.
> Always, the sudden lull
> At the top where the green air
> Holds breath in its hands
> And arms walk with no elbows.
> In that still circle, a starling
> Whistles the strict sound
> Of a name: mine, a fox's, a crow's.

4   December 25: number 84. So what are you going to do?
     Christ, I don't know. Maybe I'll claim sanctuary and
     move into the Judson Baptist Church. Sleep up at the
     holy end until some bird pecks me Morse Code through
     the stained glass.

5   After Labor Day, bare pipes
     Stand footed in concrete,
     Their wings and
     Genitals removed.
     Iron steps rise from the snow
     But a child climbs to a sudden
     Emptiness.

6   If only the vowels would stop rising
     And falling, I could say it out.
     I can hear it shuffling on a spruce
     Somewhere behind my head. But
     e, *y*, and *i* wobble on legs too thin for a bird.
     I cannot give my name.

7   Night.   Children race
     In a ring, one fox, two geese,
     Till the spokes blur
     And the red and black of the wheel
     Throws numbers into the trees.

Calling her sister's name
Clear as the moon, a girl
Ducks into the still hub.
Then daughters spin out from the rim,
Slivers of words in the Christmas snow.

two

The sea breaks. I turn
And take it, a monk's
Hood over my head,
Then dive into a wave,
Feeling the heave and slough
As tangled water passes.

Out beyond breakers, water swells
And settles, taking a deep breath
For the landing. Buoyed by this depth
I let all sinews go, sell these bones
To the sea—two good shoulders
And a bad leg. Let water take

Them, salvage or discard them
As it will. No time but this.
No obligation, no comfort, no
Accomplishment. No person but
The sea with its cold hands. The sun,
Too far, touches no part of me.

Without my willing it, the sea
Brings from its hoard a salt recollection:
The bitter ache for a daughter
Dead, a girl who walked weightless
In my love. Her absence rises
And falls with me in the heavy water.

Shouts from the beach. Another girl,
Alive, runs to taste the cold
In a single dash and fall.
She swims out, and I crawl
Over the curl of breakers
Toward the lame and slippery shore.

A Thin Song
for a girl

Your eyes
Worry with words
And the curl of
Numbers, fearing
A wrong turn.

I wish I could say
Unlearn them—
The world's skin
Is unlettered
And n is no
Count.

I wish I could say
The rain erases
Numbers and
Rinses names
Away.

           But
It would not
Be true. A stand
Of oak speaks
With ten thousand
Green tongues
Scattering words
Like a blur
Of blackbirds.

Even Brushy Fork
Multiplies and
Divides on its wet
Slate.   The dark
Marks will be there,
Mumbling their mysteries.

Forgive them
If you can.
Already you know
Round numbers
By their tuck and roll.
Behind the bars
Of a lined page
You know a mean
Wind by its
Garlic breath.

Pry invisible bits of green
Off the rocks and lift them,
Delicately, to the moving flame
Of their mouths.   They nibble grain,
These sea-sparrows,
Their song the thin click of claws.

The ocean keeps its distance.   Then a fuse
Burns white, right to left across
The water;   the beach smokes and roars
Breaking the big news
Even on this distant county.
After the spume, the rocks are empty.

Out of a crack, a red leg tries the silence—
Then scores of legs.   The crabs are back.
Everyone samples the lettuce, and the rock
Honors the reticence
Of shells that bow sideways and do not speak.
It honors the courtly elbows of a dance.

1   Above Colorado, clouds drift toward us
But their shadows lie still,
Lakes pressed in the brown land.
Soon clouds must reel in
Line and draw the shadows
After them. But for the moment
They float westward, neglecting
The heavy water.

2   I hiked a mesa this morning, with friends,
Checking a ponderosa pine to see
If the red tails had returned. We found
Petrified wood, pebbles of lava in the sandstone,
A cow's pelvis, white, in a shallow cave.
Lunch on a flat rock, and sun.
I supposed what was dazzling
Had to be brief. But those mountains!

3   Nebraska. Sea horses
Rear out of white coral,
Whorls and loops of the ocean
Floor. Further east, clouds
Flatten. Here and there
A mound rises pinkish above
Drifts of old snow.

Iowa. Tumbled grey, the open
Dome of a brain. I imagine
A long electrode probing,
Probing for the pleasure
Center lost somewhere
In that dark cauliflower.

4   On the prairie, a coyote cries once
Far off and drops into the wide, dry bed
Of a river; a magpie snatches away a dead
Sparrow. Compulsions keep their distance.

My toe pressed a pane of ice
This morning in a hollow rock,
Water curling up from the edge to lick
The sun. I was almost weightless,

Lifted by the balloon of my own
Breath. That is a country of eyes
And imagination. A cloud lies
Down with a mountain, mimicking his humped stone.

But touch hung empty at my side.
My hands remembered the curved bark
Of another landscape. Now I wish
This plane down into the close salt and seaweed;
I speed the earth's turning, hurrying dark.

5   The Mississippi curls her
Deep body around Burlington.
A splotch of lights
Shows through the clouds—
An even purple now, edged
With a pale orange line.

6   Come, love, fish in this lake
Of your own making, the dark
Water of my body.

I am short of breath
From the altitude, coming
Near you, dropping into O'Hare
Field, 17 degrees and snowing.

One puts together
A face
Working it up out of scraps
Of leather, pitch, cornhusks,
A knot of weeds, even orange
Peel or the rind of walnuts.
The lucky ones find a bit
Of clay or limestone.

Often it comes out well—
A remarkable likeness.

Making it sometimes takes years.
The trade is passed down
In families and countries,
But training is not everything.
You, on the first try, have turned
Eye, forehead, throat,
To a discipline
Beyond the skill
Of journeymen.

Feet

Two fish in a river, chewing
Gravel with their five
Fat teeth.   First one
Moves ahead
Then the other,
Frightening crawdads
Behind rocks.

"Wonderful, wonderful," say the feet,
Strangers to the slippery green water.

Belly

Muscles are logs lying
Under the white water,
Dangerous for travellers.
Belly button is a whirlpool
Where the blood spins down.

Arm

By day it is a spear
With a fish on each tine.
By night, a   tree
With five white leaves
Stirring in a hungry wind.

Hair

It waves at strangers.
It looks back to see who is following.
In the water, it grows upward like seaweed,
Searching for a green sun.

Skin

At night, skin is the first to sleep,
Slipping into the water,
Pulling elbows in after it.

No, skin never sleeps.   It flies
Like a martin over the water,
Catching mosquitoes, listening
For the sound of breath,
Dodging the dark branches.

For Katharine, 1952-1961

I
Your flesh is melted, I suppose,
To Indiana clay. Only your bones
Attend that deep box. Graceful
They must be, even now.

II
Dead as many years
As you lived. If a child
Grows back down, a year
For a year, you are a hard
Birth to be taken in,
A conception, and nothing.

III
Katharine, we die.
My father is dead
And his brother.
Some of us grow down
While we live.
                    What?   Am I telling you
About death?
                    This is what I know:
You visited the neighbors'
Cats. In the park, you
Climbed down rocks
To fern and twisting
Water. Once we camped
By a soggy little lake, drove
Home in the rain, late,
Singing, the lights of the towns
Blurred and wonderful in the wet

Pavement.   We planted
Corn, do you remember?
And in August felt
The full ears, husked
Them, broke the sweet
Kernels with our teeth.

You grew so easily
There seemed no other way.
Your voice held out
Its hands, palms up.

This motion, this poise—
Broken to wet bones in a box.

IV
On this day of your death,
We love.   The steep
Water of your making
Is still green—
And will be, will be.
The fern, the falls,
The keeping on.

September 1971

three

Sonnet
declining to write confessional poems

Left to myself, I flatten to clear water,
Giving back gray-green rocks, low
Clouds, a lighthouse that marks the slow
Traffic of a gull and a freighter.
I breathe wild onion cut by a sickle bar
On shore. The mower cools a beer in shallow
Water, leans for lunch on a shadow
Whose shape is mine. I have no character.

Must all songs twist out of the conches of our
Ears, roaring the inward salt and blood?
The real sea keeps a dour
Beat, scraping what music it can out of flood
And ebb. It never asked me to pick
A sea riff on the five strings of my neck.

Harry Houdini
Belle Isle Bridge, Detroit, November 27, 1906

We curled the cold air over our heads,
Kept hands in our pockets.   You stood
Against the grey Windsor sky
And jumped from the bridge, naked
Except for trousers and two
Pairs of police handcuffs.
The black water eddied and sucked.

One minute, twenty-nine seconds.
You surfaced, waved
The irons, and swam to a boat.

Later, the story improved.
You jumped through the ice, you said,
And, pulled downstream by the current,
Lost the hole.   Tilting your head
You breathed between ice and water,
Searched in widening circles for the air.

The truth is enough.   You leapt
And a dog howled on the bank.
The Detroit River, which has never refused
Anything, refused you.
Threw you out, clean and cold,
Unlocked, out of the downhill
Lurch of Detroit water.

Jennie clomped on stage,
Ten thousand pounds they say
And you can well believe it,
Lumpy elephant standing
In those four wash buckets
Of feet.   They opened
The cabinet, front and back,
And turned it to show us:
Empty right through.
Jennie walked around, then in.
Houdini raised his arms
Like a preacher
And fired his pistol.
When they drew the curtain,
Nothing.   Ten thousand pounds
Vanished.   Blue ribbon around her neck,
Alarm-clock wrist watch
On her left hind leg,
Gone.

I felt the Lord moving in me
The way He moved in Jennie,
His hand on my shoulder.
I shouted, "Praise God.
He is taking off my flesh.
I am like to fly.   Praise the Lord."
My body vanishing, the flesh melting
Upward into the air.

But Houdini stopped it. "Go back
To your body," he said. "It is not yet
Judgment Day. Go back to your body,
Madame." And fired the foolish pistol again.
He couldn't stand a real miracle.
So I went back. Flesh in its sack of skin
Slung from my shoulders. Jennie was gone,
Ten thousand pounds, but he wouldn't let me
Shed my sackful.

                 The room went heavy.
Arms, buttocks, breasts hung
Fat as sausages across the chairs.

Harry Houdini
Digger's Rest, Australia, March 16, 1910

You are showing off, Houdini, that scarf
Around your neck, at dawn, at Digger's Rest.
Goggles. Waving to Bess from the mad
Machine. You brush the top branches
Of a gum tree, then rise—flying.

First flight on the continent.
It took twenty-three seasick days
To get here, hungry for that record.
But this is your record, Houdini: you act
Everything we dream. Coffins,
Rivers, keys moving in locks, the binding
Of wet sheets. They were ours
But you have taken them. Falling,
Drowning, hanging in air. You fire
A pistol, pull a knot of cloth until a room
Fills with gold, green, orange, purple, red.

Now in your Voisin you bank against the wild air
Of Australia, our fears and longings
Streaming after you like gaudy silk.

I
Wind behind the eyes. My head
A blown egg.
Nobody here but a jay
And the rubber sting
Of cars across a valley.

The yolk ran out
At my mouth,
The white at my nose.

Now I am light in the hand
And float
On any water.

II
That woman with landlord's lips
Rages
Shakes me into broken English.
Lion heads where you lay your hands.
Her nerves. Her rights.
Her furniture. Daddy.
Daddy. Claws in my neckbone,
Acid on my tongue.

My room rises,
Runs its string to a dead
Tree in Minneapolis,
Lodging cockeyed in the branches.
Ants dig in at the corners,
An ugly boy pricks
Me, my skin mouldy
As cheese. Dirty
Veins. Bad blood.

Daddy, when milk sours
You pour it down the sink.

III
Spring comes
With its sweet mouth. Three
Weeks ago, the Mississippi
Trumpeted, heaving up ice
On ice. Today leaves
Unfold and a lame wind
Has its way with the water.

Cold was better.
This air on my neck,
I gnaw trees
Till the sap runs
Down my chin, put
My knee into
The refrigerator
To keep it from melting.

Mother spreads the thick
Smell of her men on the underside
Of the rug. Their
Calf skin gloves fall
Limp on windowsills and
Doorknobs. Outside, the stupid
Grass tilts its lips
Up to tires and boots.

This water music:
A downspout hawks rain
From its throat, spills it
To a black lake
Between houses.

Still convinced that things may be done right,
She waves a cane,
Conducts a tuneless band of maids and cooks,
Her family.   Unwilling

Players, they fall silent, sullen.
Judgments hang
In the air like the smell of sauerkraut—
Nothing to discuss.

(Outside, a wind changes the light from grey
To green to rose
And shuffles the feathers of birds
On a telephone wire.)

They wonder: would it matter
If children threw
Open a window and a sudden air
Blew persons

Out of place around a dinner table?   If curtains
Flew?   If the postmarked
Letters of her name were stirred
To a gentle disorder?

It would matter.   Like a great owl,
Her will
Digs talons in the flesh of her neck
And pulls her straight.

Above her, above them all, its wings
Tear the flimsy logic of the wind.

Plentiful as blackberries, reasons hang
From the foliage of the head, round,
Faultlessly formed, ready for plucking.
I will present them to you, a double hand-

ful, from no other motive than love.
These are cultivated ones, large
As grapes. Try them. Never mind the tough
Fleshed seeds you find below, lodged

In the underbrush. Wild pears or pignuts.
Let them lie. Many botanists contend
Those are not true reasons at all, but a genus
Apart. Besides, they are difficult to find

Being tangled, often, in vines and roots.
Neither edible nor decorative. GET YOUR HANDS
OUT OF THERE. Forgive me. I meant to say these,
The blackberries, these are my reasons.

Elbows on the walnut, she cups
Her face in her hands, watches
Balls explode from the racked
Triangle. Her tail waves thoughtfully
Like the butt end of a cue.
She blues the velvet tip, cradles
The stick between thumb and forefinger,
And strokes. The two ball
Drops and the three
Sidles up to the side pocket.

Any woman can ease the cue
Back along her hip and send
The white ball clanking.
But will the four drop? The five?
No. Not even if she lifts
Her knee and twists her shoulder
Left across her breast, helping
The ball home? No. The art
Is calculation. Geometry of incidence
And reflection. Cushion to cushion.
It asks an eye for angles
And a sweet touch on the polished stick.

Strangers took you
For a nice old lady
Until, speaking foolishly,
They walked into the sidelong
Snick, snick of wit
Across logic. You read
Henry James and stock
Reports with the same
Deliberate eye, allowing
Words to give themselves
Away. Intelligence
And generosity. A honey locust
Grew in your yard, thorns, fine
Pinnate leaves, white blossoms
All over the street.

Now you go to the dark
Station near the old inter-urban
Tracks to buy a ticket
To the other Greencastle.
"You're *in* Greencastle," they say
And refuse to sell.

Tools

No one speaks of the Craftsman tools
He polishes in his surgeon's shop.
Planer? Sander? Saber saw?
What sort of crowbar
Will he lean on to pry this hollow hip
Out of its socket?

I see the bone man smile
Like a Sears ad, big face and open collar,
Arms hairy among the chips
And bonedust. His fingers
Confide in the ground steel
Of the knife.

Adultery

White and red. The bone curves
Voluptuous in his professional
Eye. Launcelot of calcium. Casanova
With auxiliary tools.
I pay this cool hand
To visit the sweet
Blood of my blood, bone
Of my bone while I am absent.

I foresee the event:
The big man swaggers in
Loosening her garments,
Fondling the most private turns
And crevasses.
                    Woman,
You have reason to wonder
At my complicity.

Flight

Done. Strung with ropes. Wired up,
A bi-plane banking and looping
Over a cornfield.
                    I watch
Calm as a farmboy
To see if the bragging pilot
Will nick a windmill and burn
In the alfalfa.

Cleaning the Fish

A fish flat on a board.
Gills heave on this slab,
Sour work for a fishwife.

Itch

Ripped off an acre of tape
To expose an ecstasy of itching.
Oh, the deep indulgence
Of scratching, the tender skin
Crying for more, even as it
Breaks and bleeds. Pleasure
Beyond the most exquisite eating
Or drinking, beyond
A naked dive into the cold
Water of a quarry.
Rub against the sheets, massage
With hospital lotion,
Scratch.
Dig in to the knuckles. Pain
And pleasure like love
In the sweet briar. More,
The skin cries, More.

The big handed lover
Neglected to write this spasm
On the chart. The itch
Has given my body
Back to me.

Cattle

Vertical. Moving again.
Down the corridor I wave
To all the poor cripples,
Showing off. Placing a crutch
On the foot pedal, I catch
The water cooler at the top
Of its arc, then wipe my mouth
On my shoulder, glancing
Back, signalling the other cattle
To follow through the break
I have discovered
In the electric fence.

Steel and Bone

One day I will go with hardly a limp.
Still, the steel squeaks and sighs
Against the bone. A horseshoe
Nailed to a tree and overgrown
By bark. Planted, it will
In time grow steel ankles, steel
Elbows, steel balls. A heaviness
Already troubles the joints of my tongue.
I will race my daughters again
But I carry a cold sound
In my hip pocket.

four

Perched on the handlebars, you are living
Backwards, pedalling the wrong way,
Pulling left for a right turn.

You are writing
A crooked poem
From the bottom
Up, not even
Turning
To see where
It will start.

A stranger rises like heat from the pavement
To fill the empty spaces.   The boys
At the Gulf station remember his license plates.
When he walks up the hanging street
Past the bank and the barber shop,
Dogs feel the pull of air and follow him.
Without saying a word,
He grows larger than any of us.
When he crosses the street, we drive
Between his legs, honking and staring up.

A boy sits crosslegged
In a low cave, the pupil
Of a half-closed eye.

Junior Powell, Sand Gap, Kentucky
with a borrowed guitar

He picks a fast passage, waking
December flies on the ceiling.
Listens.
Tunes the first string, low

High low. Tries an A chord,
And D. He picks his passage again
Untangling it
From the strings, offering

That ornament to a bare room
And a long night. That riff is his
Employment.
He winds two strings down

And up again. One of them whines
Lost. He smiles. Worries the knob.
Nothing here
To tune by. Outside a pile

Of coal squats in the path
Blocking the way. He tries D
Building it
From the bottom up, sixteen inches

On center, a life. The top notes
Falter and warp. He winds down
Three strings
And starts over. Smiles. Uncertain

Intervals hollow out the time,
A vacancy between drops of rain.
You know
How to tune this son of a bitch?

Jimmy knows but he's gone.   All tunes going
Or gone, roads turning back
On themselves.
You know how to play poker?

We play five card draw with no money, showing
Our hands after the draw.   A pair of fives
Takes it
If there was anything to take.

With a single line
You draw from flat water
The face of a catfish.

The boat's shadow crossed
By a catfish. Brown on brown—
We float on that art.

High wind, high water.
Teach me to hold on
Crow, cockroach, catfish.

Sprinkling and Immersion

I look in the wrinkles of these hills
For a new life.
Can the sprinkling of December rain
Drown the old body and raise
A ghost of fog out of damp rocks?

Let it be immersion
Falling back into the full
River, all the way
Under, silt, slate, and water—
Then the shouting for one rinsed
And wrung, handshakes, hugs,
The gift of a strange tongue.

Daylight runs down the black
Legs of the trees, disappearing
In a mulch of leaves.   South
Of town, Brushy Fork collects
What light is left, hunching
Its shoulders over the cold trickle.

Rust

Mountains kneel to drink
Humping their backs over cupped hands.
Whatever sits still
On these lovely slopes
Corrodes
And whatever moves
Must find its own gait
With no instruction
But the running of the rain.

Ocean

We will start again in a fair climate—
On the ocean where we can trust
The rise and fall of our salt blood,
Where our children will boil seaweed
And clams over a wood fire
And need no friends. But then
The signing of deeds, the packing
Of our ailments in a green bag
And strapping it to our shoulders.
It will be worth it: a landscape
That buoys us in on its breakers.

Every year, the pause before a new
Beginning, a new life suspiciously
Like the old. Bad actors, we play
Ourselves in a new location,
Wading ashore like heroes
Through all the water
We have passed or washed in.

Going Back

Going back to a garage that smells
Of fertilizer and motor oil

Or to an upstairs room where
You lay awake to the rain
And the moving cars—

Going back, you do not expect
Pleasure. You hope to find

That words broken open
Spill on a dry tongue
A taste they have been saving.

You hope to find
Water still cold as iron.

East Pinnacle

The girls leave for school, and the sun
Comes up in orange smoke over Big Hill
And Sand Gap. The door opens
To spring in December.
We discover we have made
No promises. No one will miss us
If we walk out to feel the breast
Of a mountain tighten in the cool light.

We climb a gulley where rain
Has followed the path of a porcupine
Crosswise and down.   A titmouse
Cleans the air with his teetering call.
The forest has dropped its leaves;
Now it listens and waits.

Suddenly a pileated woodpecker
Rides red and black through the trees,
The plume of his flight mocking
The monkish season.   His high
Yakyakyakyakyak calls
The hillside to a hard dance.
When he drums his bill to the brown bark,
Our bodies take that deep tattoo.

Rivers

Whether it rains or not
Brushy Fork slides and sidles
Over its broad slate bed.
Water oozes from the fat
Rocks, coal juice dribbling
From the side of a mouth.
It brings no traffic
But it has studied two ridges
And a valley, and its word is good.
If you are going to Silver Creek,
It will show you the way.

*

Where I grew up, streets were the only
Rivers. After a rain, I cleared leaves
Away from the iron grate, watched
Water careen along the curb,
Plunge to the sewer hole,
And boil out of sight.

*

Knowing rivers, you know the slope and bias
Of the earth's body. You know how the land lies.

*

The only river I could name
Was the Detroit River, making
The slow commuter run from Grosse
Pointe to Lincoln Park and back.
It lapped the sludgy banks of Belle
Isle and the pier where Bob-lo Boats
Came in blowing a calliope of promises.

Flies

I take a dry satisfaction in my corner
Of this huge room: rain-stained ceiling,
Table, teapot, chair,
The enormous window where flies
Come to die.   On the sill,
A wasp strains to his knees,
His abdomen dragging, wings
Sticking out like ears.   Flies
Twitch on my paper, buzz an inch
Into the air, spin over
The edge, carrying their demons
To the sea.   December and they
Still die;   the floor is crisp
With bodies.   I believe they die
Of boredom.   The glass of this window
Offers nothing but light,
Their hairy feet hungering
For the steam of manure, swill,
Wet flanks, udders.

Flies, if Easter ever comes,
We will rise together and buzz off,
A man in a black cloud
Hunting fresh sweat and honey.

Culvert

Brushy Fork moves
Over slick shale, picking
The scabs of fallen trees, narrows
To the black hole of a culvert
Where its coughing echoes
Back on itself,
Matter deep in the throat.
But always moving. Under the dry road
Water rattles in the corrugated pipe
Until coughing settles into
Something like health—a meadow,
The gentle seepage of cow dung.
Not pure. Not your New Hampshire
Brook. But moving. A new smell,
Strange land under the flowing body.